THE JOB LANDING MINDSET

HOW TO SHIFT YOUR MINDSET TO LAND YOUR DREAM JOB

LISA RANGEL

CONTENTS

ISBN: 978-1-7333176-1-0

DISCLAIMER: While the author has used her best efforts in preparing and producing this ebook, she makes no guarantees, representations or warranties with the respect to the accuracy or completeness of the contents of this book and specifically disclaim any implied warranties for sale for fitness for a particular purpose. No warranty may be created or extended through affiliate or marketing partnerships in print or online sales and marketing materials. The advice and strategies contained herein are the opinions and based off client experiences of the author and may not be suitable for your situation. You should consult with a proper professional where appropriate. The author shall not be liable for any loss of profit, income or commercial damages, including but not limited to special, incidental, consequential or any other damage.

INSPIRATION: COUNT ALL THE WINDOWS

When I was a business development manager for a recruiting firm, I was responsible for finding job openings at other companies that my firm could then fill for them.[1]

My territory? New York City.

Yes, the city that never sleeps, naps or even blinks.

It's on all. the. time.

It's ruthless territory.

The competition never sleeps, naps or blinks either.

However, I was *good* at my job—consistently #1 or #2 in my company.

Most days, I would sail out to the subway and into my next client meeting knowing I had the goods and the team to best service a company's needs. And I would often land a job assignment for me and my team to fill.

Other days, though, I was dejected, overwhelmed and felt consumed by the competition.

Like I would never land a job assignment again.

My team and I would starve.

I would get fired.

Those were crappy days.

Here's how I turned myself around on those dark-minded days: I'd go to the top of a tall building. I'd pay to go into the Empire State Building, or go to the Marriott Marquis restaurant at the top of the hotel, or choose between the myriad of public building tops in the city.

And I would gaze at the vista of buildings spread out before me and say to myself, "Count all those windows..."

See, behind each of those windows was an office.

A potential buyer.

Someone I could try to get a meeting with and pitch my services to win them over.

An opportunity was behind each one of the hundreds of thousands of windows I was looking at in the majestic landscape view before me.

And I only needed one sale...

Just one.

So, when you're feeling overwhelmed by your job search and start thinking that no-one wants to hire you, or that the competition is inching out ahead of you, or that you'll never land a job...

Just remember: you only need one job.

So look at the Fortune 500 List.

Take a gander at your LinkedIn connections.

Think of all the people your connections know, and how many people the connections of your connections know.

Review the Inc. 500 company list.

Peek at college alumni lists.

Look at Best Places to Work lists in your area.

Lists in industry news publications can be a source of inspiration.

With all so many possibilities in front of you, have you reached out to all these people and companies yet?

I'm thinking probably not.

In these lists lie windows of opportunity.

You only need one job.

You do not need to solve the unemployment or

underemployment rate in the United States. You do not need to come up with a solution for the talent shift around the globe.

You do not need to fix all the economic problems you hear about in the news.

You only need one job.

And you have a vista of company and contact windows to choose from.

Turn yourself around by looking at the windows of opportunity before you.

Pick one window and start there.

That's all you have to do.

That's all you have to focus on.

Ignore the other noise... and look out at all the windows.

1

A JOB-SEARCH WARNING FROM ROCKY BALBOA

Have you watched any of the *Rocky* movies? You know that feeling when the song *Eye of the Tiger* starts playing—like you can conquer the world?

Well, *Eye of the Tiger* came on when I was at the gym, and this line jumped out at me: "So many times, it happens too fast... You trade your passion for glory."

This got me thinking about what it's like when you climb the corporate ladder and hit the top ranks in your career: it happens fast and you trade passion for glory.

At least, that's what happened to me...

In fact, it happened to me twice in my career when I reached the point of reporting directly to the president of a small company.

As I hit my stride getting to that level, the promotions, accomplishments and accolades poured over me.

At first, it was awesome. I felt like a rockstar, enjoying the glitzy perks and glamorous paycheck that came with a high-level role.

I put in long, hard hours and I was rewarded.

But once I'd been in that high-level role for a while, something strange started to happen. At least it did for me. Once I started up the ranks, the glory was great. But often, my passion didn't rise up with me. It's a confusing predicament to be in and no-one really warns you about it.

I interviewed very successfully for each promotion I received, but with every step up the ladder, I unknowingly started to focus less on my career passion, and more on obtaining glory and yet another feather in my career-cap. And, because I started simply going after the titles, I became less and less satisfied with my work.

I would reach the pinnacle and think, "Is this it?"

My achievement seemed empty to me.

And I did that *twice*.

I realize now how common it is to drive for the glory carrot and forget about the passion—we think the glory will be enough to fulfill us.

But I am here to tell you it isn't.

After about three or four months, the novelty of a title and higher paycheck wears off. If the passion isn't there, you can feel empty.

I'm not saying you should resist your urge to chase achievement or accolades or glory because you're *definitely* going to lose passion for your job if you do. What I'm saying is, despite the fact that you never quite know how your career is going to unfold or how quickly you'll rise, you can interview specifically to ensure you'll have passion in your new job or promotion.

If you want to know how to land a job or promotion on your terms that align with your values, or better prepare yourself for your next performance review, you need to know what your values are and what makes you tick.

What if I told you it's possible to have passion *and* glory?

Well, you can...

The fact that you're reading this book is evidence that you're open to doing things differently.

Start by listing activities that make you happy or, if you're struggling to figure that out, ask yourself, "What used to make me happy?" Focusing on what makes you happy makes you a more desirable candidate.

Once you've done this, hold on to that list and read on...

THE UNSEEN BEAUTY OF YOUR EXECUTIVE CAREER

I love visiting places where artists create. Artists of any kind—in no particular genre or medium.

During a trip across Europe, I had the pleasure of visiting a number of places where famous artists created their work.

Some of the places I saw were:

- The mundane building where David Bowie met a British singer named Vince Taylor, who was the inspiration behind Bowie's infamous Ziggy Stardust persona.
- The beautiful waterlily ponds at Monet's farm in Giverny.
- And the deplorably conditioned apartment and office space in Paris where Ernest Hemingway resided and worked.

Even though I've seen other artists' spaces throughout my life, I walked away this time with something I'd never really considered before.

I realized that up to this point, I believed great masterpieces were created by the artist who saw something incredibly riveting, which then inspired them to create their art.

When in actuality:

- Vince Taylor was supposedly a whack-job and David Bowie met him in a downtrodden bar/cafe—one would not describe that as inspirational.
- The waterlilies at Giverny are ordinarily beautiful. Not *extra*ordinarily beautiful. Need proof? Even though beauty is in the eye of the beholder, Google "waterlily pond—Monet" and you'll see pictures of other waterlily ponds that I believe most would describe as equally as beautiful—making the Giverny waterlilies just ordinarily beautiful.
- And Hemingway's office and apartment, during his first stint in Paris, was a five-floor walk-up roof dwelling that lacked heat and, in some places, walls. We would describe it in modern times as gross.

Yet these artists created masterpieces from these ordinary sights.

You might be thinking, "Well, duh, Lisa, of course, they were uniquely talented artists with a gift."

But I don't think it's that simple.

In fact, I left inspired with this concept:

Art is about appreciating and highlighting the beauty right in front of you.

I think too many people wait for the right inspiration. Or the right opportunity.

Those people are wrong and they are missing out.

Instead, it's about creating masterpieces with the ordinary views and tools in front of you.

Right in front of you.

When I had this epiphany, I felt so empowered.

Our masterpieces are *right* in front of us.

Each one of us.

Don't believe it?

On this trip, my daughter noticed a Monet painting. I can't remember the name of it, so bear with me.

It was a simple landscape painting of a river flanked by land with small plain buildings on the sides of the river and a clunky steel bridge over the river. It was so peaceful and pretty, but a plain landscape.

So plain, my daughter said, "Mom, this painting looks like it could be the bridge I row under on the Passaic River[1]."

She was right—it did!

The point is, Monet created beauty out of a scene that genuinely looked like it could have been from urban New Jersey. Clearly, it was in rural central France—but we see what we see.

Why am I telling you this?

When you think there isn't beauty in your own background, I'm here to show you how to look at yourself from a fresh perspective.

Most of us are ordinary, accomplished executives and professionals. But there is beauty in the ordinary. Masterpieces can be inspired by what we see in the mirror and in the world right in front of us each and every day.

5 PRINCIPLES TO ACHIEVE CAREER HAPPINESS

E mployers really only want to hire happy people.
They don't want to hire the baggage you're carrying because it may get in the way of you doing your job. It's a heartless world and we're just living in it, right?

NO! It's not.

The world is not heartless and you *deserve* to be happy.

I know what you're thinking: "Easier said than done, Rangel..."

But it's doable. I am not in the "easy" business.

I am in the "get it done" business.

And I view career happiness as something worth working for.

I get happiness done.

Want to know how? I'll tell you right here and now. Just keep reading.

My 5 Principles to Achieving Career Happiness are as follows:

1. Forgive your colleagues when they screw up. Forgiveness doesn't make it okay that they screwed up, but it releases you from the resentment.
2. In an absence of information, don't fill in the blanks.

Understand you may not know everything that's going on. See someone get away with something at work that they should have been reprimanded for? Well, don't assume because you didn't see them reprimanded that they weren't reprimanded. It's none of your business, really, and it's only distracting you.

3. Accept that people are doing the best they can—even if you don't like it or it's different than your best. Assuming everyone is a screw up or not trying as hard as you is a terrible way to go through life and will surely make you unpleasant to be around. This doesn't mean you can't have standards—it just means you don't have to be a demeaning jerk about it.

4. Realize people are not seeking out ways to screw you. Victimhood and persecution complexes are very unbecoming in new hires.

5. Depend only on *you* to promote yourself and no-one else. Even when asking people to promote you—follow-up and have a back-up plan. Ultimately, everything in your career is dependent on you. No-one else is responsible for your advancement.

See? It's clear what you need to do.

Now that you are—or soon will be—happy, it's time to find that new job. Let's do this.

4

ARE YOU LETTING PEOPLE LIE TO YOU?

My personal trainer friend shared with me that when she welcomes new clients onboard, she asks them to tell her their goals. Many of them actually say things like, "I would like to lose 10 lbs this week. I have a wedding coming up."

Grown-ass, professional, educated adults write this nonsense down. **#smh**

My friend says, "If you want to lose 10 lbs this week, I'm firing you as a client. It's not possible in any way without putting your health at risk."

She is a true professional.

Most of the time, her clients stay and follow her realistic, albeit long-term, plan. And they let out their dress a little for the wedding, or go buy a new one...

But the yahoos that leave her office in a huff?

Those clients *will* find a trainer who will "listen to their client" and co-sign their BS and take their money. Then, when the training plan doesn't work in a week and they have a health risk, they will blame the trainer.

And the trainer *should* be blamed.

But doesn't some fault lie with the client who firmly believed the unrealistic premise in the first place, and didn't heed the advice of professionals telling them otherwise?

In the job search world, some of the signs of a delusional job seeker[1] are the beliefs that:

1. A resume will land me a job.
2. I don't really have to network since I have great experience. Someone will want me for what I do and how I do it.
3. I can find a job in a month (even though I've been at my company for 17 years, making $175,000, and don't really have a network).
4. I want a career change aged 54 to do something *really* different—but no, I can't take a pay cut and, in fact, really need an increase (because employers always want to pay people more to learn something new... <sarcasm>).

See what I mean?

There are some nonsensical notions that jobseekers at all levels tell themselves to feel good.

And there are unethical job search coaches and resume writers who will co-sign the BS you tell yourself to take your money.

Some people let "experts" lie to them—and pay for the privilege.

Don't be that person.

Be open to the truth, not just what you want to hear.

Follow the advice of a pro who will tell you the truth, particularly the truth that you don't want to hear.

Be open to the hardcore truth of what is holding you back.

Don't let people lie to you anymore.

Seek truth about yourself. You will land a job faster when you face the truth sooner.

And you will have more control and confidence about your next steps—and less cause to worry.

5

OVERCOMING YOUR EXECUTIVE CAREER "WALL OF WORRY"

F inancial newsletters and media outlets have been talking about the bull market climbing the "Wall of Worry." I understand this to mean the bull market continuously climbs despite political, geographic, and economic worries plaguing the news and influencing these markets every day.

You can Google "bull market climbs wall of worry" to find stories all over the financial news outlets.

I lived and survived in the market crash of 2008 and the stock market plunge in 2001. I worked for an NYC company whose second largest client was Bear Stearns in 2008. Not pretty.

Each of those crashes was preceded by a Wall of Worry.

So, are we destined for an imminent financial crash? I have no idea. If my market predicting abilities were half as good as my job landing abilities, I would be a trader instead of a resume writer.

However, I do know that what goes up, comes down. And what goes down eventually comes up. The only security during these tumultuous swings is to be prepared for whatever the world throws your way.

Would your company survive a massive client loss?

Would your job be crucial in weathering a downturn—or would you be the first to go?

You'll want to be prepared for whatever comes your way if you don't have career-preserving answers to these two questions.

Want to be extremely ready?

Have your resume, profile, job landing plan, and interview prep ready to go—ahead of time, at a moment's notice. Don't wait until you have to act and then scramble to get everything together.

Job security isn't found in one job or one company.

Job security lies in your ability to always find a new job at the same level fast.

Could you find a new job fast, if you had to?

If you hesitated at all answering that question, and if the answer is anything but an emphatic, "Yes", think seriously about getting help to become ready.

Your job security is at risk. But you can minimize the risk.

You can conquer the Wall of Worry and reach the Palisade of Career Peace. Here are three ways to do this:

1. Write a SWOT Analysis of your current situation (Strengths, Weaknesses, Opportunities, and Threats).[1]
2. What is the one topic/question you hope interviewers don't ever ask you?
3. Make a list of 10 people you could call who could help you in your career.

Now, share that list with us at lr@chameleonresumes.com with the subject line "Mindset Book 3 Item List" to discover which are the best next steps for you—and beat the job search paralysis that stalls so many talented executives.

6 SIGNS YOU'RE SUFFERING FROM JOB SEARCH PARALYSIS

B efore we go on, let's make sure you're in the right frame of mind to search for your dream job.

Whether it's been 10 years or 10 months since you last looked for a new executive position, you'll find the whole process to be a much different and tougher experience than the last time you looked for a new job.

Perhaps you've done everything in your power to learn about social media and the online job hunt… but unfortunately, there's tumbleweed and you're getting nervous.

That can cause us to stall. It happens to everyone at some point. The crucial thing is to get you unstuck.

Start by using this guide to determine if you're showing any of these signs of job search paralysis.

1. Hiding behind your computer instead of talking to people

If you truly know everything about this new job hunting world, but you're still hearing crickets rather than your phone ringing (or your inbox filling up with interview requests), then something is off.

The reality is you may have plenty of knowledge, but you're

paralyzed when it comes to taking action. Ask yourself—and answer honestly—whether you've been proactive on the job hunt or just waiting for recruiters to contact you on LinkedIn.

Even though there are tons of online tools to help you with your job search, the truth is: you need to take action to get anywhere. This may include reaching out to hiring managers directly (look beyond HR and search firm recruiters), attending networking events, or following up with individuals within and outside your network.

Many job hunters fall into this trap when it comes to using online tools for the job hunt—they forget to talk to people. Or, they think they don't have to talk to people because social media will take care of it.

Nothing could be further from the truth!

Personal relationships get people hired, not social media views.

2. You believe profile views, likes and social media shares will result in job offers

Social media will only get you so far. Start with small steps on social media—but you must follow up with action like a phone call, email, or an active instruction request.

Social media alone will not land you a job; it's simply a tool to help you find the right opportunity and to help opportunity find you. Simply "being on LinkedIn" will not land you a new job... you must work these tools to generate opportunities.

Despite what you may hear from so-called social media experts, passive communication alone does not result in job offers. In fact, it's in your best interest to combine online and offline marketing strategies to yield the best results.

3. Job boards alone will yield a job offer

Like social media, job boards alone won't yield a job offer. In fact, many companies don't even post jobs on massive job boards— especially not for the kind of high-level positions you're looking for.

You have to go the extra mile in a couple of ways.

1. Check out a company's corporate website for job postings and their application process.
2. Actively seek out contacts in HR and online outside of HR through emails, phone calls and in-person follow up at conferences, conventions, and networking events.

4. You've rearranged your resume, cover letter, and profile ad nauseam

There comes a point where there's nothing else you can do with a resume or cover letter. You can only rearrange it so many times.

Endlessly focusing on the details is a way of unconsciously avoiding taking action. The "never-ending resume tweak" is a form of procrastination preventing job seekers like you from putting themselves out there.

If this sounds familiar, you may want to rethink rearranging your resume and instead focus on getting out there, talking to contacts, and meeting people.

5. You're worried about privacy

If you're still worried about privacy in this day and age, you may need to get with the times. It's not that privacy isn't important; it is. But our lives are all online already anyway.

Nobody is suggesting you put your social security number online —and if you have genuine safety issues to contend with, then be prudent. But realize that every privacy measure you take against possible bad events happening could also keep good events (like interview calls) from happening, too. Strive for the right balance.

Furthermore, recruiters want to know as much about you as they can before they get in touch with you. It's not just about skills any more, it's about the person.

6. You're concerned people will see you as a pest, so you don't reach out

If you're not introducing yourself or following up with contacts, you're leaving money on the table. Period.

One way to combat the idea of feeling like a pest is to realize that you're being of service to the recruiter or employer by letting them know someone with your skills and abilities is available. You have the skills that can solve their problem—and as such, it's your duty to let them know about it.

Do any of these signs of job search paralysis resonate with you? Be honest. If you are experiencing job search burnout, read on to discover what you can do to fix it and get the job search results you want and deserve.

7

THE PARALYZING FEAR OF LOSING WHAT YOU HAVE

I remember my last year at a job I'd been in for nine-and-a-half years.

I was burnt out on my company.

I was burnt out on the recruiting I was doing.

I was *really* burnt out starting up recruiting offices.

But I had a good gig. A *fantastic* gig.

I had well-paying job expenses, too. I was locked into the job—or so I thought.

Because mine was the sole income in my family. Hubby was a fabulous stay-at-home dad. How on earth could I leave?

I wasn't looking at the bigger possibilities outside my company; I was terrified and focused on losing what I had.

This mindset paralyzed me for a number of months and stopped me from doing what I really wanted to do: move on and grow.

What did that paralysis look like?

This paralyzing fear took the form of:

- Working through lunch.
- Hiding behind all the work I had to do.
- Taking on more work I didn't have time to do, then staying later to do it.

Was it self-imposed self-importance?

Nah... I hid behind the work. I hoped that doing the work would speak for itself—and speak for me, instead of owning the fact that I had to sell myself. I came to the realization that I couldn't depend on my work alone speaking up for me; nor could I depend on mentors speaking up for me. I had to speak up for myself and sell my assets and accomplishments to the decision-makers

The denial was exhausting.

Luckily, I snapped out of it. With a little help from a friend, I started connecting with colleagues who had left their current employer and started networking.

I found these contacts using LinkedIn.

I started having meetings.

The meetings led to more interviews—and my next job.

Woot woot!

But I did more than just find old colleagues on LinkedIn; I made new connections and target lists of people I wanted to connect with.

So start calling prior colleagues.

At the minimum, you may start to shed that fear of losing what you have and start to see all the possibilities that await you.

Once you've identified those possibilities, it's time to start going after them. And to do that, you need to think like a marketer...

DO YOU THINK LIKE A MARKETER IN YOUR JOB SEARCH?

A re you waiting for recruiters to call you with a job opening?

Trolling job boards hoping the right job surfaces?

Then scrambling to throw your resume and cover note together so you can submit it via the online portal—hopefully capturing a smidge of a recruiter's glance?

Then there's the wait to find out if you managed to get an interview... and realising the whole thing is an exercise in how to waste time.

These are some of the ways accomplished, well-paid executives are looking for their next well-paid leadership jobs.

Does this sound like the action of a strong, capable, confident leader?

Does this sound like *you*?

You're an accomplished person who's worked insanely hard to climb the corporate ladder. Perhaps in the past you've had to elbow competitors out of your way to land in a coveted position.

Your entire career, you've looked like a winner at every turn—and now you're looking for that ever-more elusive high-level role when you're at your highest salary and least flexibility.

I mean, who wants to work 90 hours a week any more? At this point, it's about working smarter, not longer and harder.

Do you really think you'll find that dream role on a job board? Maybe. Possibly. Along with lots of other people all hoping for the same thing.

Don't depend on a job board to post the right job for you to grovel over and then scramble to apply for.

Don't wait for some recruiter to call you with a job opening that might be a fit—because chances are it's been pitched to two dozen executive grovelers already.

Does this sound like the behavior of a winner to you?

If you've hustled to win throughout your whole career, why would you now take the passive approach?

Why would you stop the hustle, when it's never been more important?

You want to finish the last 15-20 years of your career on top, right?

So don't depend on the pedestrian job boards or wait for the elusive-could-win-the-lottery- feeling-dispenser, aka the third party recruiter, to call you.

You can make these interviews happen for yourself— just like you've made everything else happen in your life: by taking back control.

What if I told you that you can learn how to create your own opportunities like a professional marketer, to generate your own job leads?

Are you making yourself easy to find?

Not just on job boards. Are you being effectively active on LinkedIn, attending conferences, doing professional development, publishing your insights, joining industry members groups?

Are you positioning yourself as the kind of person your future boss is looking for? The kind of person who's perfectly suited to your dream role?

Think like a marketer and market yourself directly to decision makers in the hiring process. That's how you land interviews.

If you have a sitting duck mindset, and you're waiting for people to call you or for job posts to appear, you will not be successful in your search. Someone else market themselves into your dream role, and you won't even realise you've missed out.

Start to think and act like a marketer. Take back control of your job search and generate your own interviews.

You will have interviews if you do this. No doubt.

So don't wait another minute: stop the struggle. Either you go pick up the phone to start making connections or you call us for help so you can learn how to make this happen.

Do either now.

1. Pick up the phone and call the connections who can put you in touch with the right decision-makers.
2. Book a call with my team right now and we'll show you how to make it happen: https://chameleonresumes.com/contact-us/

AVOID THESE 6 REAL JOB SEARCH MINDSET KILLERS

E veryone knows the job search can be a stressful time marked by hopeful ups and defeating downs.

You get excited about new leads and, sometimes in the same day, suffer disappointments on your hunt for that perfect job. This is normal.

Remember it's normal, because if you don't accept it as part of your job search, you could become your own worst enemy. You may start taking it personally.

Without even knowing it, you could be throwing up resistance that will kill your job hunt success. This resistance takes the form of physical mistakes and emotional baggage, and it hampers your ability to land that great new job.

Whether you're a top-level executive looking for your next big advancement in an already successful career, or you're a recent college graduate seeking that first job to kick off your career, you could be guilty of throwing up emotional roadblocks that will stop you in your tracks and prevent you ever setting foot in the door of the kinds of companies you want to work for.

There are many common mistakes job seekers make when

looking for that next big job. Here are the six I see most often among candidates:

1. Research Fails

Often, candidates believe they're well-prepared for their interview by researching all they can find about the company—but they don't research the company's needs and history. They then fail to align their strengths to what the company needs.

This can cause a candidate to flounder in the interview, and erodes confidence in that and future interviews.

2. Talking Down Accomplishments

During the interview, many candidates seek to appear humble and often talk down their own accomplishments. This can make it seem like they really didn't do anything in their past employment.

Be proud of your accomplishments. Pride isn't the same as arrogance. Talk about your achievements, and balance them with humility so the interviewer doesn't perceived you to be boastful.

3. Going It Alone

Job seekers often feel they must pursue their next job like a lonely hunter in the night. The truth is, you can get a lot of valuable information and learn something useful from others in your position. Talk to people who can help you.

Seek out the help of recruiters, colleagues in similar positions, and job search experts—but don't rely on them as your only source of new opportunities.

4. Begrudging Attitude

No-one likes searching for a new job. But your attitude to the job search is crucial. Approaching it with a bad attitude only results in poor quality work on your part.

Be excited about your new opportunity and enjoy the hunt as you broaden your horizons. You may even learn a thing or two along the way.

5. One-Size-Fits-All Resume and Cover Letter

One of the biggest mistakes you can make is sending the same cover letter and resume to many different companies. If you're truly interested in a position, do your homework and tailor both your resume and cover letter specifically for that position.

6. Negative Head Trash

The biggest emotional and mental drain at the root of a stalled job search is assuming all setbacks are unique to you and happen only because you're not a desirable candidate.

It's important to realize *all* job seekers have positive and negative experiences while they search, and this is normal. Setbacks do not mean you suck. A negative experience simply means that employer and job opportunity was not the right one for you.

Remember, when you're job-seeking, look at your actions objectively.

Look deep inside yourself and ask why you're having a hard time. Ask why you're not finding the type of job you want. You may discover it isn't because you simply can't find something, but that you've become your own worst enemy and you're creating unnecessary resistance in your job search.

Don't be too hard on yourself. We're all guilty of negative self-talk at one time or another. Just pick yourself up, recognize what you're doing, and correct it.

HOW YOU HANDLE CAREER SETBACKS IS WHAT MAKES YOU UNIQUE

A ldous Huxley said, "Experience is not what happens to you; it is what you do with what happens to you."

Everyone thinks their situation is unique, but it almost certainly isn't. We all suffer from similar setbacks and find ourselves in similar situations.

Here are three examples of calls I've had with prospects.

1. The Emergency Resume Call

"I have a unique situation. My dream job appeared! I'm interviewing in two days and I don't have a resume—can you help me?"

Answer: Yes, but you're not unique. I had one other call just this week with someone who had a dream job interview fall into their lap, and they weren't ready either.

2. I got a job—and then they pulled it! Help!

"My situation is different. I was promised a position under the newly merged company, since I'd built up the previous two products we had. I stopped my interviewing and focused on the new job coming, and they just pulled it from me. They told me I don't have a place in the newly merged firm. So now I'm scrambling to find something. Can you help me?"

Answer: Yes, we can help. However, channeling my inner Yoda, I'm here to tell you: "Unique, you are not." I had two other people in the same week reach out to tell me their company's plans for them shifted, and they're not getting what they were promised.

3. The company suddenly closed!

"You are not going to believe what happened to me. Company closed down our location with no notice. Just like that... I mean, have you ever heard of such a thing?"

Answer: Yes, I have. And it's not unique. And we can help.

I can give you even more "unique" situations that people experience every day.

Here's the one thing we all have in common: we all have career setbacks.

We all have adverse experiences; the kind of thing we'd rather not talk about at cocktail parties, and that we'd certainly prefer interviewers not to ask about. Every single one of us.

Here's where you make yourself unique: it is what you *do* with that experience that sets you apart from the crowd.

Whatever lemonade you make from those lemons is what draws the crowd of lemonade drinkers who want to buy the yummy drink you're selling.

THE SECRET A-Z ATTITUDE IMPROVEMENT TRICK

W e've all had days when we wake up on the wrong side of the bed. Don't get me wrong: I truly *love* what I do. But sometimes we have those mornings where our head is not right. Can you relate?

Yeah...

I recall one particular morning when I got out of bed and shut the alarm off, my lower back was aching and I cannot remember what I did to make it throb in such a way.

The kids were not getting ready as fast as they should, putting me behind schedule.

I was annoyed by the coffee not perking at the speed of light—and not entering my system intravenously or, better yet, by osmosis.

One glance at the inbox on the phone told me there were already 23 emails in before 6:45 am.

And there was more, but I won't bore you with the tedious annoyances that piled up: traffic, breakfast not fully cooked, first appointment was late, etc...

What was different about that morning was I could not shake it off.

Early morning faded into late morning and still I could not shake the bad mood.

In hindsight, I probably needed to be sequestered away from people for the day. I laugh about it now, but I know some people I spoke to that day would agree with me.

It was about noon and I was still in a mentally bad place, so I called a good friend of mine. I vented about all that was ticking me off that morning.

I knew in the big scheme of life what was irking me wasn't even a real problem... it was simply logistics not going my way.

But I still could not shake the bad attitude from my head. It was not going away.

So my friend said to me, "Alright—listen. Go grab a piece of paper."

She waited for me to grab a sheet of paper and a pen then continued, "Now write the alphabet down the left margin... one letter per line."

I'm thinking, "What?" But my friend is a tough-love girl like me, so I just did what she told me.

A B C D E... all the way to Z.

"Ok," I said. "Now what?"

"For every letter, write something you're grateful for that begins with that letter. For example, for me, my grandmother's name is Adelie, so I would write Adelie next to the A. I love bananas, they make me happy, so for B I would write bananas. It doesn't matter what it is: a person, place, situation, thing, concept, institution, feeling, whatever—just write it down if you're grateful for it."

I say what I'm thinking, "Um, I do not have time to come up with 26 items that are letter specific."

"Well," she said, "you had time to call me and vent about what's putting and keeping you in a bad mood, so how about you spend some time on an exercise that can improve your attitude?"

My shoulders slump down and, like a child, I reluctantly obey.

That afternoon, I started writing my alphabetized gratitude list, starting with A.

I did go out of order a bit; some letters were easy: the names of my kids and husband went next to those respective letters. I was slowly forgetting they moved too slowly early that morning.

I was certainly grateful for the coffee—despite the fact that earlier on I was irked by it not entering my system fast enough. I wrote coffee next to "C".

X... X... X...

What do you write down for X?

Hmmmm: the Xtra cheese I put in my omelet that morning (which caused it not to melt all the way through because I was rushing).

I was grateful for the warm bed I woke up in that morning (I put this under W). Grateful for the cool clients we get to service each and every day (that went under ???)

I was grateful for the automobile I sat in while in traffic (yes, I used A for this one instead of C for car, since coffee went under C).

I was grateful for my parents being still relatively healthy, for having the best staff on the planet, and so much more.

After about 35 minutes, each letter had a word next to it. This made me feel better.

It changed my attitude in an afternoon.

I recommend this exercise anytime you need an attitude improvement.[1]

Your family, friends, and colleagues may appreciate it.

12

DO YOU FEEL "STUCK"?

I regularly talk to job seekers who tell me they're "stuck".

They wait until they perfect the language on their resume before they send it out, and they keep asking for feedback for different people.

They get different feedback every time, so they're in constant resume-editing mode—but they never contact anyone about interviews.

These job seekers want precisely the right list of contacts to reach out to before they even start reaching out. They want to have their interview preparation down pat—yet they haven't sent out a resume.

Here's one of the bigger "stuck" scenarios: a job seeker is worried about getting an offer at a company he's not entirely sure he likes. A recruiter saw his LinkedIn profile, was interested, and gave him a call.

And the job seeker hasn't called back or even submitted a resume yet.

Although I feel honored that people trust me with these stories, it pains me to hear them.

I can feel the pain and frustration each person experienced as they told me their story: always assuming things have to be perfect before moving forward.

Worrying about a problem they didn't have yet.

But we want progress—not perfection. Perfection is paralyzing. And it's subjective.

If you're chasing perfection, you're chasing something that's different for everyone.

But here's the best news: you are already perfect.

Stand with that knowledge. Send what you have.

Reach out to just one person to start with. And then the next person. And then the next.

Do as much research as you can to prepare for an interview and know that you, as you are, are enough.

If you get an offer you don't resonate with, you can always turn it down. That's a great problem to have.

I tell my kids: you're always going to have problems. Always. So go get good problems, not bad problems. An offer you don't want is better than no offer.

Some interview prep with a confident stance is better than too much prep and stressed out—or no prep at all.

Sending out an awesome resume and making valuable connections is far better than making your resume perfect (whatever that is), not sending it out, and not chatting with anyone.

You get unstuck by doing the next thing in front of you imperfectly. Not to pull the Nike tagline, but: "Just Do It!"

Getting unstuck starts with one action.

I know you can do this one action. Let's go.

Action: List 15 people from your LinkedIn connections, college alumni, and corporate colleagues who could potentially help you find your next position. Reach out to at least one of them today. Then do the same tomorrow, and the next day.

13

YOU'RE NOT A VICTIM SO TAKE CONTROL

I had a year-long ChamTriber ask me what I thought of an article about discrimination towards the unemployed.

He is a skilled, experienced tech person who's been unemployed for a year and he was curious as to what I thought about efforts to make the unemployed a protected class (which has been successful in some capacity in some states in the US).

My answer?

I don't pay attention to it and I think focusing on proving it or disproving it is a waste of time. It won't land a job seeker a job.

Let's say discrimination against the unemployed (which means not interviewing someone who is currently not working because the employer assumes they have dated skills, are lazy, or are unemployable in some way without evaluating each person) is 100% real.

Let's assume that we prove beyond a reasonable doubt that such discrimination exists and is the sole reason why this Triber is not employed right now.

What does that do? How does that help?

Can you take that proof, take that "win," and go collect a paycheck somewhere?

No.

All this proof does is justify a victim position—oh, poor you, you can't find a job because of unemployment discrimination.

stroke your hair... there there...

You can't even buy a cup of coffee with that sympathy.

Spending time researching this type of thing, proving it, and justifying it simply wastes valuable time you can spend doing activities to *land a job*.

After a few emails back and forth, here was my final response

You have been on my list for about a year. Have you read my other posts? I always say don't go through recruiters or HR. Third-party recruiters are paid by companies to find specific talent. They get parameters from their clients who pay them and deliver candidates with those requirements to get paid. And yes, companies don't want to pay a fee for unemployed candidates they can get on their own. They want the hard-to-find, fresh-to-the market talent for the fee they will pay.

That's not discrimination, that's economics.

Luckily, only about 10% of hires happen through recruiters. Around 70% of hires happen through networking. However, you can reach out to 50-100 directors of IT who, being IT people, may see your potential and bring you in to train you for those positions that need a few days of training. An HR person is directed to find a certain set of parameters. An IT director will see potential.

I've been writing about this for the past year and you have been on the list. Ask yourself these questions:

- How many IT directors have I reached out to directly? How many IT networking events have I been to?
- Of the IT directors I reached out to, how many of them have I reached out to more than once when I didn't hear back from them the first time?
- And, if I did reach out to 50-100 IT directors, and didn't

land a job, did I find another 50- 100 to reach out to...
and am I determined to that until I find a job?
- How many school alumni have I reached out to in the
spirit of networking? Have I attended any school
networking events recently?

Any time spent researching whether or not unemployment discrimination is real is not productive. It feeds victimhood, in my opinion. So I don't have a comment and I'm not an economics expert. I know I have seen people who are unemployed for two years get work by doing the above and I have seen 17-year stay-at-home parents who have regained employment at the level they had before going out of the workforce to raise their family.

And none of them found work depending on a recruiter.

Does unemployment discrimination exist? Probably.

But your choices are (1) to accept that it exists and continue to reach out to the wrong people, research articles that justify the belief that you are being discriminated against, and remain unemployed.

Or (2), even if it's 100% true, say, "Screw it. I'm going to be different" and stop using the same tactics that aren't working. Quit researching articles that justify your victimhood. And then do what I mentioned above.

You only need to find one job. You don't need to solve the world's unemployment problem. So stop approaching recruiters. If that's not working, try something new.

Good luck.

I say the same to you.

If you have a victim mentality about the obstacles you experience, today is the day you stop this mentality.

You will now view this situation as a problem that needs solving so you can find the one job you want.

We become what we think about most and we begin to resemble the people we spend the most time with. So change what you're putting into your brain and surround yourself with people who are positive action-takers.

Action: Start changing the narrative today by listening to job search experts who can help improve your mindset and give you the best chance of finding that dream job. Sign up for daily career tips here: https://chameleonresumes.com/get-daily-career-tips/.

14

THE MOST IMPORTANT SKILL YOU NEED TO SUCCEED

P eople don't believe me when I tell them I was a quiet little workaholic in my 20s. Well, they believe the workaholic part... but never the quiet part.

I was afraid of everything. And I worked so hard to overcompensate for all my fears.

I worked the longest so no one would think I was lazy.

I worked the hardest so everyone would see me as a dependable "result dispenser."

I made sure I always had a solution because I wanted others to always know that I worked smart.

But I never told anyone I worked the longest, or the hardest, or the smartest. I just did it.

And I expected my boss, co-workers, and other managers to see that I was rocking it... and recognize me accordingly.

But they didn't.

Well, they sort of didn't.

When there was additional work to be done, I was always "recognized" (you know that feeling, eh?).

And when there was a promotion available, I was always *not* recognized.

#insertsadlisaface

I'm not suggesting the person who got the promotion didn't always earn it on their own merits (sometimes they didn't deserve it, but other times it was a deserving person).

Whether the person did or didn't deserve the promotion wasn't the issue. The issue was that *it could have been me.*

If I'd spoken up about my wins, my working smart, hard, and long hours, and the results I brought... that promotion could have been mine.

But I didn't speak up and the promotion was not mine. I was about 27 or 28 years old when I realized what the problem was.

I realized I had to learn how to sell my abilities and influence others to my point of view. No matter what I decided to do in life, I had to learn this skill.

I had to learn to sell.

I realized, then and there, that I could not depend on other people selling me, even if they believed in me.

Even if I didn't stay in sales my entire life, I had to learn how to sell someone on my ideas, on hiring me, on joining my team, on giving me funding, on my way of doing something.

I realized sales was a life skill.

So I took a job where I had to learn how to sell—or I'd get fired.

I took a job as a commission-based recruiter in a bullpen office environment with just me, my phone, and a computer at my desk.

My desk was up against 20+ other desks alongside other recruiters, and I made calls from 8 am until 6 pm.

Me—shy, people-pleaser, do-what-you-ask-to-make-you-happy girl—sitting in a bullpen with mostly aggressive recruiter dudes (and a few aggressive chicks) in a Wall Street financial recruitment office.

If I wasn't making calls, everyone saw it.

If I sounded like an idiot on the call, everyone heard it.

If I did not make my numbers, I would not have the honor of dialing for dollars at my desk with my phone and computer any longer.

There were some days I swore I was on the brink of tears.

But I would not cry in front of the recruiter dudes and chicks (I would save that for the short, infrequent bathroom trips).

I was going to learn how to sell, damn it!

"I can do this," I would say to myself...

And I would listen to other people make calls. I would listen to sales tapes. I would write my scripts over and over until I was comfortable using the tactics in my words.

And I sold... I sold my face off.

Then I got promoted—four times in the next nine-and-a-half years—maybe even five if you count the time I did two jobs simultaneously for seven months until others were hired.

Promotions (and subsequent new jobs) happened not because I worked harder, smarter, or longer than anyone else... promotions (and new jobs) happened because I sold myself and my skills. I worked my network to find opportunities to sell myself.

I depended on my network for introductions, but I never depended on them to sell me. I sell me.

And now I teach people how to sell themselves and how to create opportunities to sell themselves.

No matter where you are in life, if you can learn how to sell you, you will create demand for yourself.

Always.

Once you learn this skill, you won't ever look back.

15

TURN YOUR PASSION INTO A CAREER... OR SECOND CAREER

Today's economy forces you to look at where you are and what you're doing. Working for a sizable pay-check or for notable prestige alone isn't fulfilling enough for most people during challenging times—or anytime for that matter.

We want—heck, we *need*—to feel internally fueled by our work.

Turning a passion into an intrinsically rewarding and financially sustainable career is the dream of many, yet only a few truly achieve it.

Here are some steps you can take to start turning your passion into your next career move—followed by the steps you need to take to make it happen.

Identify your passion and find the resources to pursue it

Non-Profit Volunteer Pursuits

I've worked with clients who have made the shift from a corporate role to a cause that was near and dear to their heart.

Have you always wanted to work for a company that funds cancer research? Or medical research to help children with autism?

You can use your skill set and passion to work for a cause that internally motivates you to achieve. If you're an accountant, you can work for a cancer research non-profit in the accounting and finance department. Do you have a talent for managing staff and identifying talent? Apply your human resources expertise to an HR role or a membership development role within the non-profit cause that lights a spark within you.

Hobbies

Love to run? Figure out how you can translate your corporate skill set to work for a sports organization that focuses on running for your next employment gig. Or research how to start a running group as a side business venture. Not all passion pursuits need to evolve into full-time employment.

Perform a search in LinkedIn Groups using the keyword "running" and you'll find plenty pertaining to marathons, half-marathons, and other running enthusiast groups. Review the backgrounds of group members for leads and connections: do they work at companies that support an aspect of running (apparel, vacation tours, events, sports advertising)? Do these connections work at "regular" companies with an active runner contingency outside of work?

Use LinkedIn Groups to help build your network and engage individuals with common interests. Then see if you can transform those interests into a career path or join a corporate culture that aligns with your passion outside of work.

Corporate Work in Companies that Inspire You

If you have a natural talent and interest in digital marketing but want to leave your stable, conservative corporate marketing job, consider a role with a funky, aggressive startup that serves small and mid-sized businesses. You can use the LinkedIn Company Search function to locate and pursue boutique marketing firms with a small employee population or upstart revenue stream.

You can also conduct search for "digital marketing" within the LinkedIn Skills & Expertise Section to identify jobs, companies, and connections that are affiliated with digital marketing. Look at related skills in this section to identify other areas of passion to pursue, to ensure your search and pursuits are thorough.

For example, when looking at related skills for "digital marketing" you'll find you can consider mobile marketing, digital strategy, or online lead generation as concepts to incorporate into your passion-focused job search.

You may realize you have a more marketable skill set than the one you initially focused on, or you may have a stronger interest in another area with a skill that can be easily cultivated.

Culture & Worldly Travels

Have a passion for history? Travel? Have you considered being a tour guide or working in the tourism industry abroad? You can use search engines and LinkedIn resources to identify companies that run different types of tours in locations where you've always wanted to live.

Reach out to new contacts you discover through your research to learn more about working in these industries. Talk to people to find out what lifestyle and financial changes you may have to make in your life to make this career shift work.

Perusing LinkedIn Groups can help you build your network and engage with individuals who are knowledgeable about your chosen passion. They may be able to help you figure out how to parlay it into a career venture.

Approaching companies and contacts who can benefit from your passion and skill set

Once you've identified organizations and connections that can help you in your quest to land a career rooted in your passion, the next step is to make contact. Conduct exploratory conversations with key individuals to learn all you can about transitioning into this area.

Your exploratory questions and conversations should elicit the following information to help you decide how to structure your new pursuit to fit your lifestyle and financial needs.

- Follow your target companies on LinkedIn and other social media to learn as much as you can about the culture and nuances of the industry and organization.

This information will help you make an informed approach at the right time.

- Sign up for email newsletters or RSS feeds to receive updated information about networking opportunities and trending topics in your area of passion. Learn as much as you can from these sources.
- Set up a communications strategy outlining how often you'll reach out to contacts within and outside your network to further your exploration and pursuit of this career path. Activity metrics will help you stay grounded and enable you to accurately estimate your efforts.
- Open your mind to how this new pursuit may manifest itself—it may not immediately be in a direct hire position. Consider consulting assignments, entrepreneurial ventures, and volunteer opportunities to start.
- When approaching companies, outline in a cover letter how your passion qualifies you for consideration. Show the reader how your skill set is transferable to this area that inspires you. Keep it concise and to the point.

Don't get discouraged. Stay the course. Anticipate that your idea to shift careers to an area that energizes you may not be welcomed by your target firms, friends, and family at first. Continue to improve your qualifications and keep networking to spread the message of your dream. It takes only one person to believe in you and give you a chance to enable you to make the change and work within your passion.

Don't give up on your passion or yourself.[1]

16

HOW TO PROPERLY CARE FOR YOURSELF WHEN LOOKING FOR YOUR DREAM JOB

I f you've lost your job or you're just entering the workforce, you could be in for a long journey as you search for that perfect job. During this process, it's important to manage your life and take care of yourself so you always look and feel your best when you land an interview.

1. Be prepared for the long haul

In today's world you won't land a job in a week unless you're very, very lucky. In fact, you could be in for a long search for your next place of employment. While few studies have been done, some experts believe it can take approximately one month of job-hunting for every $10,000 of your expected salary.

This time-frame can be affected by many different factors including your location, the current state of the economy, and much more. Do make sure you prepare yourself for the extra time, though, so you don't get discouraged if your job hunt takes longer than you'd like.

2. Be your own manager

Just as if you were at work, you need a manager to keep you on track as you search. In this case, you'll be your own manager for your job of finding a job. Set realistic goals for yourself and stick to them.

For example, decide how many resumes you want to send each day and be sure you send exactly that many before you quit for the day.

3. Keep to a schedule

It's easy to let yourself slide while you're out of work. In fact, this can be dangerous to your mental wellbeing as well as your job search efficiency.

When you begin your job search, set a schedule. Decide exactly when you'll do the work of applying for jobs. Think of this as your work schedule and be sure you stick to it.

This will help you keep to a routine, which will increase your overall happiness and satisfaction and help you be more productive.

4. Exercise regularly

Exercise has been shown to help increase not only your physical health but your mental health as well. You'll be sharper and you'll have more energy to get more done—and you'll be better able to craft the perfect resumes and cover letters to send to prospective employers.

5. Set aside time for family

Just because you're job hunting doesn't mean you don't have time for your family. Your friends and family can give you the support you need while you work. And they can help lift you up and recharge your batteries while you continue the often difficult task of finding a job.

6. Groom yourself as if you had an interview today

Now is not the time to become a hermit. You may not have somewhere to go every day, but you still should take the time to properly groom yourself. Treat each day like an interview day and try to look your best.

If you look good while you search for work, you'll feel good about yourself—which will help increase your confidence and happiness.

7. Don't let the negative feelings takeover

During your search for work, you will be rejected over and over again. It's normal and it happens to everyone. A long string of rejections can leave people feeling stressed and discouraged.

You must not dwell on these types of negative feelings as you continue on your job search. Stay positive: it's the key to good overall health and you'll stay motivated to find the perfect job.

8. Invest in yourself

Just because you're out of work doesn't mean life has to stop. In fact, this downtime is a good opportunity for you to invest in yourself. You'll undoubtedly have a little extra time on your hands while you're out of work, making it the perfect opportunity to do a few things for yourself.

This doesn't mean pamper yourself with frivolous luxuries you may not be able to afford; instead try taking a class or learning a new skill. This will keep your mind active and help you further develop your set of skills and improve your mental health at the same time.

It could even make you more attractive to a potential employer.

Looking for a new job can be daunting, especially if you're currently out of work. Don't give up, even if you've been rejected.

Stay positive and follow these steps to take care of yourself so you have the confidence you need to tackle your next interview with relative ease.

17

HOW EXERCISE CAN ENHANCE YOUR JOB PERFORMANCE

E xercise has many more benefits than enhancing what you see in the mirror. Yes, it can help you get in shape so you look your best, but there are many more than just physical benefits to exercise. Studies have even shown that exercise can help you perform better at work.

DISCLAIMER

Before I go any further, understand that I am not a fitness professional of any kind and this is not intended to be fitness advice for any individual.

I am the Queen of #neverstopstartingover for the amount of times I have stopped a fitness program and then started again. I'm simply sharing my own experiences and the observations of my clients' experiences when incorporating exercise into job performance.

Before beginning any exercise regime, consult with your physician first. Thanks!

Benefits of Regular Exercise

Now the disclaimer is out of the way: there are many benefits to exercising regularly. Once you get into a good workout routine, you'll soon begin to feel better and you'll find you have more energy.

It'll be easier to sleep and long sleepless nights will become a thing of the past.

Your physical appearance will begin to improve as your body begins to get fitter, increasing your confidence in all aspects of your life.

These are benefits I've experienced personally, and I have seen clients experience them too.

If these benefits weren't enough, your mind's emotional wellness also receives a much-needed boost from regular exercise. People who exercise find it easier to concentrate. They show improved memory, they learn faster, and are more creative.

On top of that, people who exercise tend to have much lower levels of stress and their overall attitude is much more pleasant as people who exercise are generally happier than those who avoid exercise.

Enhanced Physical and Mental Performance

Whether your job requires physical exertion or not, you body will be ready for any task you can throw at it. Your mind will also be at its best and ready to tackle the work you have to do each day.

Studies show that our mental power and health are directly linked to the physical exercise we do each day. Someone who exercises is able to focus more on their work and makes fewer mistakes because their mind is able to stay in the game. Exercise has also been shown to help improve time-management skills, which will improve your ability to complete assignments on time.

Emotional Benefits

Anyone who's ever worked a full day in an office environment—or any other type of work environment for that matter—knows that mood greatly influences performance.

When you exercise regularly, you'll feel better and your stress levels will reduce, improving your daily mood. These effects can go far beyond productivity: many workers feel more satisfied with their jobs and happy with their performance levels if they exercise.

Other Beneficial Effects

If you've ever put in a full day at work, you'll be familiar with the post-lunch crash. Sometime in the early afternoon your brain turns to sludge and you just can't focus on anything. Your productivity falls and you find it hard just to get through the rest of the day.

People who exercise, on the other hand, have more energy. That extra exercise-induced energy enables you to power through the post-lunch crash, or bypass it altogether. This raises productivity levels through the entire afternoon and such people usually finish the day strong.

Add Exercise to Your Daily Routine

With so many benefits to job performance, it's a wonder that more people don't make exercise a priority. The most common excuse I hear is they just don't have the time.

The truth is, though, that most people don't consider exercise important enough to make time for it each day. With a little planning, you can find the balance you need so it's easier to include exercise in your daily routine.

1. Make it fun

You don't have to bore yourself to death on a stationary bike if that's not your bag. Find physical activities you enjoy and book them into your schedule on a regular basis. Perhaps you enjoy sports like tennis or team games; or maybe hitting the pavement for a nice run outdoors is your thing.

2. Change your view of exercise

Instead of viewing exercise as a personal indulgence only to be done if there is extra time, consider it as an investment in yourself and your career. Remember, you perform better when you exercise so it makes sense to include it in your daily routine. It'll be better not just for you, but also the company who employs you.

3. Find a time and stick to it

Find a time that works for you to do your daily exercises. This could be in the morning or after work—or even during your lunch hour. Once you find a time that works well for you, stick with it. Block that time out each day and view it as a daily meeting that is mandatory for you to attend.

Exercise can provide so many benefits to your life at home and at work. You will look and feel better and your mind will be sharper than it ever has been if you stick to a daily exercise routine.

So before you decide to skip your next workout, remember what it can do to help your performance on the job. It might just help you go that extra mile to receive the big promotion you've been after to help you advance your career.

18

HOW LIFE-WORK BALANCE CAN HELP ADVANCE YOUR CAREER

M any people assume companies couldn't care less about life-work balance[1].

On the contrary, many companies are now trying to make sure their employees are healthy, happy, and balanced. As a result, they want to make sure any new employees they take on (or anyone they promote) embodies these same characteristics.

The reality is that only by being a balanced employee can you attract a truly balanced employer.

Below you'll find some reasons why companies want balanced employees as well as an explanation of how life-work balance can help advance your career. These are all ideas you can implement at the office and at home.

Start hitting the gym again

If you've been thinking about getting healthier you can now add another reason to the list: companies know that healthy people help make them profits.

Think about it: healthy people take fewer sick days, look good, and have a lot of energy. More specifically, companies know that unhealthy people cost them money on their bottom line. To put it into numbers: unhealthy employees cost companies $1.1 trillion in lost productivity.

Many companies have tried to combat this loss of productivity by implementing healthy initiatives that encourage employees to take care of themselves, like lunchtime yoga or run clubs.

As a bonus, we all know that exercise helps us deal with stress, an attribute that is essential for high-level jobs.

If it's been a while since you've hit the gym you may want to get yourself a new membership and stick to it.

Practice setting priorities

Setting priorities and acting accordingly not only helps you become less stressed, it also shows a potential employer that you can get the important stuff done. Multitasking actually makes people less productive, so prioritizing your work allows you to follow through on your responsibilities at your highest capacity.

You can start by ridding your schedule of anything that only makes you *seem* busy. For some, this may mean going out for lunch instead of working at their desk. For others it may require dropping committees they joined but have no interest in.

Take a look at your calendar and start getting rid of anything that's not essential.

Learn how to outsource and delegate

At an executive level you'll be expected to outsource and delegate to other employees or departments—but this is a skill that many people can't seem to master.

If you tend to want to do everything by yourself, stop it—and start asking for help. When you delegate to others you give yourself space to tackle your most important tasks for the company.

Delegation also lifts a weight off your shoulders: you realize you don't have to do everything by yourself, which is very stressful.

Delegation is a skill that hiring managers are really looking out for, so make sure to give them concrete examples of how you delegate tasks to others.

Start setting clear boundaries

Employees will oftentimes find themselves stressed and unproductive because they didn't put proper boundaries in place. For instance, maybe they have an open-door policy and people pop in at all hours of the day, causing them to lose their focus and take on too much. Or, perhaps they still answer work emails into the wee hours of the night.

Neither of these scenarios help employees get their work done and both could have negative long-term effects on their health. The only way to combat this is to set boundaries and stick to them.

To get the most out of your career, you must make sure you take care of yourself. By implementing some of these strategies you not only start living a healthier life, you also express qualities that are needed in a leader.

Action

If you haven't already done so, sign up for my daily job-search tips to keep yourself motivated and positive. You'll get daily tips to find the position you deserve, right to your inbox: https://chameleonresumes.com/get-daily-career-tips/

19

NEXT STEPS

R eading the right books and listening to the experts is a great first step—but, as I'm sure you know, information and knowledge isn't enough to get results.

It's time to step up and take action.

Work through this book, taking the action steps throughout—then take the next step to landing your dream job.

The Interview-Generating Resume Package

Create an achievement-centric resume using templates and tactics that will land you interviews and reduce your job search time.

If you submitted your resume right now for your dream job, would you get the call? How effective has your resume been so far?

Are you able to outline your professional history, successes, and skillset to capture a hiring manager's attention in just six seconds—because that's all you'll get! That's right: the average resume gets just *six seconds* of attention. Recruiters and hiring managers decide *fast* whether or not to follow up with you.

You need a powerful resume designed to cut through the noise and stand out among the hundreds—possibly thousands—of other applicants. This set of tools and templates shows you *exact* layout and language you need to use to get the attention of the right people.

Create your interview-generating resume here: chameleonresumes.com/interviewgeneratingresume/

The Brand New "Get Hired Fast!" Package

Gain access to the hidden job market and reveal unpublished positions using insider information to grab the attention of interview-granting hiring managers with this brand new package.

Are you sick of submitting resumes into the job board black hole without receiving any interview calls?

Perhaps you're unsure where to look for those lucrative opportunities you've heard about but can't find?

Do you attend interviews and think you've nailed it—but never get the promised call back?

Then this package is ideal for you.

We'll take the mystery out of how to write an powerful and streamlined resume and show you how to conduct a successful job search. We'll pull back the velvet curtain and get you "in the know" when it comes to those elusive lucrative positions others seem to known about, but are hidden from you.

Multiple offers are common with our approach: go from struggling to get calls to picking and choosing among great job offers—fast.

Get the "Get Hired Fast!" package here: chameleonresumes.com/gethiredfast/

The Executive "Get Hired" Package

If you're looking for a job in the $100K plus range, work with a dedicated recruitment expert at Chameleon Resumes to develop a custom plan that maintains lifetime employability.

The average 6-figure executive position receives in excess of 250 resumes, with the first one submitted within seconds of the job posting going live. Instead of joining the scrum to chase after jobs everyone is after, become the person recruiters and hiring managers are looking for.

We'll show you how to leverage key-word optimization and action-driven language to structure your resume and LinkedIn profile so you stand out from the crowd—and the top hiring managers come looking for you.

Apply to work with us and land your next 6-figure role here: chameleonresumes.com/executivegethired/

WHEN YOU WORK with Chameleon Resumes, we don't deliver cookie-cutter solutions. One size does *not* fit all. The last thing we want is for you to blend into the background as just another application.

We draw on our unique experience as former top-tier recruiters and human resources experts to work closely with you to develop a custom plan that maintains lifetime employability — helping you land your next 6-figure executive position and beyond.

Our team will craft your executive resume, LinkedIn Profile, and other marketing documents into powerful career marketing tools and show you the most effective job-landing activities to help you land your next position faster.

Not sure which package to choose? Contact us here: https://chameleonresumes.com/contact-us/

Have a question? Reach out to me, Lisa Rangel, here —lr@chameleonresumes.com

www.chameleonresumes.com

ABOUT THE AUTHOR

Lisa Rangel is the founder and managing director of Chameleon Resumes, named a Forbes Top 100 Career Website. She was a moderator of LinkedIn premium groups and career blogger since 2012. As a recruitment professional since 2007 and as a Cornell University graduate, Lisa has held management and producer roles in numerous companies, ranging from international recruitment conglomerates to focused executive search firms.

In Chameleon Resumes, she has assembled the best team of resume writers and job search consultants who all have prior search firm and corporate recruiting experience—Chameleon is the only firm of its kind! Lisa and her team know first-hand which resumes get a response. They've reviewed thousands of resumes over the years and helped top recruiters find talent for top organizations, working with clients in 67 countries.

Lisa is a member of the National Resume Writers' Association and Professional Association of Resume Writers and Career Coaches. She has been featured in person, online and in print on Fast Company, Forbes, LinkedIn, Newsweek, Money, Business Insider, CNBC, BBC, Crain's New York, Chicago Tribune, CIO Magazine, American Marketing Association, eFinancial Careers, The Vault, Monster, U.S. News & World Report, Good Morning America, Fox Business News and many other reputable publications.

She is the author of nine books, creator of the Get Hired Fast job-landing training series, and a serial advice giver through her website ChameleonResumes.com. You can sign up to get advice from Lisa directly into your inbox from https://chameleonresumes.com/get-daily-career-tips/.

facebook.com/ChameleonResumes

twitter.com/LisaRangel

linkedin.com/in/lisarangel

instagram.com/chameleonresumes

THANK YOU

Thank you for reading—if you've found this book valuable, please leave a review on Amazon!

NOTES

Inspiration: Count All the Windows

1. This is why we are so incredibly good at teaching job seekers how to find openings —it was how I made my living!

2. The Unseen Beauty of Your Executive Career

1. The Passaic river is in New Jersey, USA, and it's one of the top 10 dirtiest rivers in the country. And my daughter rows crew there—yeah, she doesn't jump in the river, she just rows on top of it.

4. Are You Letting People Lie to You?

1. I've written about this in more detail in this article: www.chameleonresumes.com/ 5-signs-you-might-be-delusional-executive-job-seeker/

5. Overcoming Your Executive Career "Wall of Worry"

1. This article will help: https://chameleonresumes.com/written-your-recession-ready-resume-yet/

11. The Secret A-Z Attitude Improvement Trick

1. If you want to learn more about how gratitude can help your job search, read 3 Ways Gratitude Improves Your Job Search Results: https://chameleonresumes. com/3-ways-having-gratitude- improves-your-job-search-results/

15. Turn Your Passion into a Career... or Second Career

1. You can find out more about how to land the exploratory interviews you will need to find the job of your dreams here: http://chameleonresumes.com/2015/04/ 24/exploratory-interviews-land-and-make-them-work-for-you/

18. How Life-Work Balance Can Help Advance Your Career

1. We call this a life-work balance. We believe that only by putting life first, can you start to have life-work balance.

CPSIA information can be obtained
at www.ICGtesting.com
Printed in the USA
LVHW110614010422
714992LV00005B/466

9 781733 317610